Countryside Poems

With classic photographs from
The Francis Frith Collection

Countryside Poems

With classic photographs from The Francis Frith Collection

SELECT
EDITIONS

Selectabook
Devizes

First published in the United Kingdom in 2005 by
Black Horse Books
for Selectabook Limited, Devizes

ISBN 1-84546-335-8

British Library Cataloguing in Publication Data

Countryside Poems – With classic photographs from The Francis Frith Collection

Black Horse Books
Frith's Barn, Teffont,
Salisbury, Wiltshire SP3 5QP
Tel: +44 (0) 1722 716 376
Email: info@francisfrith.co.uk
www.francisfrith.co.uk

Printed and bound in China

Front Cover: Hartford, The River and the Anchor Inn 1907 58555t
Frontispiece: Shere, the Village 1903 50269

The colour-tinting in this book is for illustrative purposes only, and is not intended to be historically accurate

THE ARGUMENT OF HIS BOOK

Robert Herrick (1591–1674)

I SING of brooks, of blossoms, birds and bowers,
Of April, May, of June, and July-flowers;
I sing of May-poles, hock-carts, wassails, wakes,
Of bridegrooms, brides and of their bridal cakes;
I write of youth, of love, and have access
By these to sing of cleanly wantonness;
I sing of dews, of rains, and piece by piece
Of balm, of oil, of spice, of ambergris;
I sing of times trans-shifting, and I write
How roses first came red and lilies white;
I write of groves, of twilights, and I sing
The court of Mab, and of the Fairy King;
I write of hell; I sing (and ever shall)
Of heaven, and hope to have it after all.

PIPPA'S SONG

Robert Browning (1812–1889)

THE year's at the spring,
    And day's at the morn;
        Morning's at seven;
           The hill-side's dew-pearled;
The lark's on the wing;
    The snail's on the thorn:
        God's in His heaven—
           All's right with the world!

from LINES WRITTEN A FEW MILES ABOVE TINTERN ABBEY

William Wordsworth (1770–1850)

FIVE years have past; five summers, with the length
Of five long winters! and again I hear
These waters, rolling from their mountain-springs
With a sweet inland murmur.—Once again
Do I behold these steep and lofty cliffs,
Which on a wild secluded scene impress
Thoughts of more deep seclusion; and connect
The landscape with the quiet of the sky.
The day is come when I again repose
Here, under this dark sycamore, and view
These plots of cottage-ground, these orchard-tufts,
Which, at this season, with their unripe fruits,
Are clad in one green hue, and lose themselves
Among the woods and copses, nor disturb
The wild green landscape. Once again I see
These hedge-rows, hardly hedge-rows, little lines
Of sportive wood run wild; these pastoral farms
Green to the very door; and wreaths of smoke
Sent up, in silence, from among the trees! …
                These beauteous forms,
Through a long absence, have not been to me
As is a landscape to a blind man's eye:

But oft, in lonely rooms, and 'mid the din
Of towns and cities, I have owed to them,
In hours of weariness, sensations sweet,
Felt in the blood, and felt along the heart;
And passing even into my purer mind,
With tranquil restoration …
                    Nor less, I trust,
To them I may have owed another gift,
Of aspect more sublime; that blessed mood,
In which the burthen of the mystery,
In which the heavy and the weary weight
Of all this unintelligible world,
Is lightened:—that serene and blessed mood,
In which the affections gently lead us on,—
Until, the breath of this corporeal frame
And even the motion of our human blood
Almost suspended, we are laid asleep
In body, and become a living soul:
While with an eye made quiet by the power
Of harmony, and the deep power of joy,
We see into the life of things.

from BROTHER AND SISTER

George Eliot (1819–1880)

OUR brown canal was endless to my thought;
And on its banks I sat in dreamy peace,
Unknowing how the good I loved was wrought,
Untroubled by the fear that it would cease.

Slowly the barges floated into view
Rounding a grassy hill to me sublime
With some Unknown beyond it, whither flew
The parting cuckoo toward a fresh spring time.

The wide-arched bridge, the scented elder-flowers,
The wondrous watery rings that died too soon,
The echoes of the quarry, the still hours
With white robe sweeping-on the shadeless noon,

Were but my growing self, are part of me,
My present Past, my root of piety.

SPRING

Gerard Manley Hopkins (1844–1889)

*N*OTHING is so beautiful as spring—
    When weeds, in wheels, shoot long and lovely and lush;
    Thrush's eggs look little low heavens, and thrush
Through the echoing timber does so rinse and wring
The ear, it strikes like lightnings to hear him sing;
    The glassy peartree leaves and blooms, they brush
    The descending blue; that blue is all in a rush
With richness; the racing lambs too have fair their fling.

What is all this juice and all this joy?
    A strain of the earth's sweet being in the beginning
In Eden garden.—Have, get, before it cloy,
    Before it cloud, Christ, lord, and sour with sinning,
Innocent mind and Mayday in girl and boy,
    Most, O maid's child, thy choice and worthy the winning.

WRITTEN IN MARCH

William Wordsworth (1770–1850)

THE cock is crowing,
The stream is flowing,
The small birds twitter,
The lake doth glitter,
 The green field sleeps in the sun;
The oldest and youngest
Are at work with the strongest;
The cattle are grazing,
Their heads never raising;
 There are forty feeding like one!

Like an army defeated
The snow hath retreated,
And now doth fare ill
On the top of the bare hill;
 The ploughboy is whooping—anon-anon:
There's joy in the mountains;
There's life in the fountains;
Small clouds are sailing,
Blue sky prevailing;
 The rain is over and gone!

from IN MEMORIAM

Alfred, Lord Tennyson (1809–1892)

NOW fades the last long streak of snow,
　　Now burgeons every maze of quick
　　About the flowering squares, and thick
By ashen roots the violets blow.

Now rings the woodland loud and long,
　　The distance takes a lovelier hue,
　　And drowned in yonder living blue
The lark becomes a sightless song …

Now dance the lights on lawn and lea,
　　The flocks are whiter down the vale,
　　And milkier every milky sail
On winding stream or distant sea;

Where now the seamew pipes, or dives
　　In yonder greening gleam, and fly
　　The happy birds, that change their sky
To build and brood; that live their lives

From land to land; and in my breast
　　Spring wakens too; and my regret
　　Becomes an April violet,
And buds and blossoms like the rest.

SPRING, *from 'Love's Labours Lost'*

William Shakespeare (1564–1616)

WHEN daisies pied and violets blue,
 And lady-smocks all silver-white,
And cuckoo-buds of yellow hue
 Do paint the meadows with delight,
The cuckoo then on every tree,
Mocks married men; for thus sings he,
  Cuckoo!
Cuckoo, cuckoo!—O word of fear,
Unpleasing to a married ear!

When shepherds pipe on oaten straws,
 And merry larks are ploughmen's clocks,
When turtles tread, and rooks, and daws,
 And maidens bleach their summer smocks,
The cuckoo then, on every tree,
Mocks married men; for thus sings he,
  Cuckoo!
Cuckoo, cuckoo! O word of fear,
Unpleasing to a married ear!

THE QUESTION

Percy Bysshe Shelley (1792–1822)

I dreamed that as I wandered by the way
    Bare Winter suddenly was changed to Spring,
And gentle odours led my steps astray,
    Mixed with a sound of waters murmuring
Along a shelving bank of turf, which lay
    Under a copse, and hardly dared to fling
Its green arms round the bosom of the stream,
But kissed it and then fled, as thou mightest in dream.

There grew pied wind-flowers and violets,
    Daisies, those pearled Arcturi of the earth,
The constellated flower that never sets;
    Faint oxlips; tender blue-bells, at whose birth
The sod scarce heaved; and that tall flower that wets—
    Like a child, half in tenderness and mirth—
Its mother's face with heaven's collected tears,
When the low wind, its playmate's voice, it hears.

And in the warm hedge grew lush eglantine,
    Green cow-bind and the moonlight-coloured may,
And cherry-blossoms, and white cups, whose wine
    Was the bright dew yet drained not by the day;

And wild roses, and ivy serpentine
    With its dark buds and leaves, wandering astray;
And flowers azure, black, and streaked with gold,
Fairer than any wakened eyes behold.

And nearer to the river's trembling edge
    There grew broad flag-flowers, purple prank with white,
And starry river buds among the sedge,
    And floating water-lilies, broad and bright,
Which lit the oak that overhung the hedge
    With moonlight beams of their own watery light;
And bulrushes, and reeds of such deep green
As soothed the dazzled eye with sober sheen.

Methought that of these visionary flowers
    I made a nosegay, bound in such a way
That the same hues, which in their natural bowers
    Were mingled or opposed, the like array
Kept these imprisoned children of the Hours
    Within my hand,—and then, elate and gay,
I hastened to the spot whence I had come,
That I might there present it—Oh! to Whom?

COMPOSING A GARLAND

Michael Drayton (1563–1631)

HERE damask roses, white and red,
　　Out of my lap first take I,
Which still shall run along the thread,
　　My chiefest flower this make I;
Amongst these roses in a row,
　　Next place I pinks in plenty,
These double daisies then for show,
　　And will not this be dainty?
The pretty pansy then I'll tie
　　Like stones some chain inchasing;
And next to them their near ally,
　　The purple violet placing.
The curious choice clove July-flower,
　　Whose kinds hight the carnation,
For sweetness of most sovereign power
　　Shall help my wreath to fashion;
A course of cowslips then I'll stick,
　　And here and there (tho' sparely)

The pleasant primrose down I'll prick,
　　Like pearls, which will show rarely.
Then with these marygolds I'll make
　　My garland somewhat swelling,
These honeysuckles then I'll take,
　　Whose sweets shall help their smelling.
The lily and the flower-de-lis,
　　For colour much contending,
For that, I them do only prize,
　　They are but poor in scenting:
The daffodil most dainty is
　　To match with these in meetness;
The columbine compared to this,
　　All much alike for sweetness;
Sweet williams, campions, sops-in-wine
　　One by another neatly:
Thus have I made this wreath of mine,
　　And finished it featly.

THE DAFFODILS

William Wordsworth (1770–1850)

I WANDERED lonely as a cloud
   That floats on high o'er vales and hills,
When all at once I saw a crowd,
   A host, of golden daffodils,
Beside the lake, beneath the trees,
Fluttering and dancing in the breeze.

Continuous as the stars that shine
   And twinkle on the milky way,
They stretched in never-ending line
   Along the margin of a bay:
Ten thousand saw I at a glance
Tossing their heads in sprightly dance.

The waves beside them danced, but they
   Out-did the sparkling waves in glee:
A Poet could not but be gay
   In such a jocund company!
I gazed—and gazed—but little thought
What wealth the show to me had brought:

For oft, when on my couch I lie
   In vacant or in pensive mood,
They flash upon that inward eye
   Which is the bliss of solitude;
And then my heart with pleasure fills,
And dances with the daffodils.

THE SCENTED GARDEN

Percy Bysshe Shelley (1792–1822)

AND the hyacinth purple, and white, and blue,
Which flung from its bells a sweet peal anew
Of music so delicate, soft, and intense,
It was felt like an odour within the sense …

The jessamines faint, and the sweet tuber rose,
The sweetest flower for scent that blows;
And all rare blossoms from every clime
Grew in that garden in perfect prime …

The plumed insects swift and free,
Like golden boats on a sunny sea,
Laden with light and odour, which pass
Over the gleam of the living grass;

The unseen clouds of the dew, which lie
Like fire in the flowers till the sun rides high,
Then wander like spirits among the spheres,
Each cloud faint with the fragrance it bears.

O ENGLISH GIRL

Austin Dobson (1840–1921)

To you I sing, whom towns immure,
And bonds of toil hold fast and sure;—
    To you across whose aching sight
      Come woodlands bathed in April light,
And dreams of pastime premature.

And you, O Sad, who still endure
Some wound that only Time can cure,—
    To you, in watches of the night,—
                  To you I sing!

But most to you with eyelids pure,
Scarce witting yet of love or lure;—
    To you, with bird-like glances bright,
      Half-paused to speak, half-poised in flight;—
O English Girl, divine, demure,
                  To *you* I sing!

THE PASSIONATE SHEPHERD TO HIS LOVE

Christopher Marlowe (1564–1593)

COME live with me and be my love,
And we will all the pleasures prove
That hills and valleys, dale and field,
And all the craggy mountains yield.

There will we sit upon the rocks
And see the shepherds feed their flocks,
By shallow rivers, to whose falls
Melodious birds sing madrigals.

There will I make thee beds of roses
And a thousand fragrant posies,
A cap of flowers, and a kirtle
Embroidered all with leaves of myrtle.

A gown made of the finest wool,
Which from our pretty lambs we pull,
Fair lined slippers for the cold,
With buckles of the purest gold.

A belt of straw and ivy buds
With coral clasps and amber studs:
And if these pleasures may thee move,
Come live with me and be my love …

The shepherd swains shall dance and sing
For thy delight each May-morning:
If these delights thy mind may move,
Then live with me and be my love.

THE HILL

Rupert Brooke (1887–1915)

BREATHLESS, we flung us on the windy hill,
   Laughed in the sun, and kissed the lovely grass.
   You said, 'Through glory and ecstasy we pass;
Wind, sun, and earth remain, the birds sing still,
When we are old, are old …' 'And when we die
   All's over that is ours; and life burns on
Through other lovers, other lips,' said I,
   'Heart of my heart, our heaven is now, is won!'

'We are Earth's best, that learnt her lesson here.
   Life is our cry. We have kept the faith!' we said;
   'We shall go down with unreluctant tread
Rose-crowned into the darkness!' … Proud we were,
   And laughed, that had such brave true things to say.
   —And then you suddenly cried, and turned away.

from THE WILD COMMON

D H Lawrence (1885–1930)

THE quick sparks on the gorse bushes are leaping,
Little jets of sunlight-texture imitating flame;
Above them, exultant, the peewits are sweeping:
They are lords of the desolate wastes of sadness their screamings proclaim …

The common flaunts bravely; but below, from the rushes
Crowds of glittering king-cups surge to challenge the blossoming bushes;
There the lazy streamlet pushes
Its curious course mildly; here it wakes again, leaps, laughs, and gushes

Into a deep pond, an old sheep-dip,
Dark, overgrown with willows, cool, with the brook ebbing through so slow;
Naked on the steep, soft lip
Of the bank I stand watching my own white shadow quivering to and fro.

What if the gorse flowers shrivelled and kissing were lost?
Without the pulsing waters, where were the marigolds and the songs of the brook?
If my veins and my breasts with love embossed
Withered, my insolent soul would be gone like flowers that the hot wind took …

SUMMER EVENING

John Clare (1793–1864)

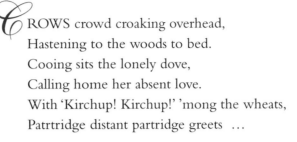

CROWS crowd croaking overhead,
Hastening to the woods to bed.
Cooing sits the lonely dove,
Calling home her absent love.
With 'Kirchup! Kirchup!' 'mong the wheats,
Patrtridge distant partridge greets …

Bats fly by in hood and cowl;
Through the barn-hole pops the owl;
From the hedge, in drowsy hum,
Heedless buzzing beetles bum,
Haunting every bushy place,
Flopping in the labourer's face …

Flowers now sleep within their hoods;
Daisies button into buds;
From soiling dew the butter-cup
Shuts his golden jewels up;
And the rose and woodbine they
Wait again the smiles of day.

JULY

Edward Thomas (1878–1917)

NAUGHT moves but clouds, and in the glassy lake
Their doubles and the shadow of my boat.
The boat itself stirs only when I break
This drowse of heat and solitude afloat
To prove if what I see be bird or mote,
Or learn if yet the shore woods be awake.

Long hours since dawn grew,—spread,—and passed on high
And deep below,—I have watched the cool reeds hung
Over images more cool in imaged sky:
Nothing there was worth thinking of so long;
All that the ring-doves say, far leaves among,
Brims my mind with content thus still to lie.

THE REAPHOOK AND SICKLE

Traditional

COME all you lads and lasses, together let us go
Into some pleasant cornfield our courage for to show,
With the reaphook and the sickle so well we clear the land,
The farmer says, 'Well done, my lads, here's liquor at your command.'

By daylight in the morning when birds so sweetly sing—
They are such charming creatures they make the valley ring—
We will reap and scrape together till Phoebus do go down,
With the good old leathern bottle and beer that is so brown.

Then in comes lovely Nancy the corn all for to lay,
She is my charming creature, I must begin to pray;
See how she gathers it, binds it, she folds it in her arms,
Then gives it to some waggoner to fill a farmer's barns.

Now harvest's done and ended, the corn secure from harm,
All for to go to market, boys, we must thresh in the barn.
Here's a health to all you farmers, likewise to all you men,
I wish you health and happiness till harvest comes again.

ADLESTROP

Edward Thomas (1878–1917)

YES, I remember Adlestrop—
The name, because one afternoon
Of heat the express-train drew up there
Unwontedly. It was late June.

The steam hissed. Someone cleared his throat.
No one left and no one came
On the bare platform. What I saw
Was Adlestrop—only the name

And willows, willow-herb, and grass,
And meadowsweet, and haycocks dry,
No whit less still and lonely fair
Than the high cloudlets in the sky.

And for that minute a blackbird sang
Close by, and round him, mistier,
Farther and farther, all the birds
Of Oxfordshire and Gloucestershire.

THE LARK ASCENDING

George Meredith (1828–1909)

He rises and begins to round,
He drops the silver chain of sound,
Of many links without a break,
In chirrup, whistle, slur and shake,
All intervolved and spreading wide,
Like water-dimples down a tide
Where ripple ripple overcurls
And eddy into eddy whirls;
A press of hurried notes that run
So fleet they scarce are more than one …
And every face to watch him raised,
Puts on the light of children praised;
So rich our human pleasure ripes
When sweetness on sincereness pipes,
Though nought be promised from the seas,
But only a soft-ruffling breeze
Sweep glittering on a still content,
Serenity in ravishment.

For singing till his heaven fills,
'Tis love of earth that he instils,

And ever winging up and up,
Our valley is his golden cup,
And he the wine which overflows
To lift us with him as he goes:
The woods and brooks, the sheep and kine,
He is, the hills, the human line,
The meadows green, the fallows brown,
The dreams of labour in the town;
He sings the sap, the quickened veins;
The wedding song of sun and rains
He is, the dance of children, thanks
Of sowers, shout of primrose-banks,
And eye of violets while they breathe;
All these the circling song will wreathe,
And you shall hear the herb and tree,
The better heart of men shall see,
Shall feel celestially, as long
As you crave nothing save the song.

from THE SEASONS

James Thomson (1700–1748)

UP-SPRINGS the lark,
Shrill-voiced and loud, the messenger of morn:
Ere yet the shadows fly, he mounted sings
Amid the dawning clouds, and from their haunts
Calls up the tuneful nations. Every copse
Deep-tangled, tree irregular, and bush
Bending with dewy moisture o'er the heads
Of the coy quiristers that lodge within,
Are prodigal of harmony. The thrush
And wood-lark, o'er the kind-contending throng
Superior heard, run through the sweetest length
Of notes, when listening Philomela deigns
To let them joy, and purposes, in thought
Elate, to make her night excel their day.
The blackbird whistles from the thorny brake,
The mellow bullfinch answers from the grove;
Nor are the linnets, o'er the flowering furze
Poured out profusely, silent. Joined to these
Innumerous songsters, in the freshening shade
Of new-sprung leaves, their modulations mix
Mellifluous. The jay, the rook, the daw,

And each harsh pipe, discordant heard alone,
Aid the full concert; while the stock-dove breathes
A melancholy murmur through the whole.
    'Tis love creates their melody, and all
This waste of music is the voice of love,
That even to birds and beasts the tender arts
Of pleasing teaches. Hence the glossy kind
Try every winning way inventive love
Can dictate, and in courtship to their mates
Pour forth their little souls. First, wide around,
With distant awe, in airy rings they rove,
Endeavouring by a thousand tricks to catch
The cunning, conscious, half-averted glance
Of their regardless charmer. Should she seem
Softening the least approvance to bestow,
Their colours burnish, and, by hope inspired,
They brisk advance; then, on a sudden struck,
Retire disordered; then again approach,
In fond rotation spread the spotted wing,
And shiver every feather with desire.

DUCKS' DITTY

Kenneth Grahame (1859–1932)

ALL along the backwater,
　Through the rushes tall,
　Ducks are a-dabbling,
　Up tails all!

Ducks' tails, drakes' tails,
　Yellow feet a-quiver,
　Yellow bills all out of sight
　Busy in the river!

Slushy green undergrowth
　Where the roach swim—
　Here we keep our larder,
　Cool and full and dim.

Every one for what he likes!
　We like to be
　Heads down, tails up,
　Dabbling free!

High in the blue above
　Swifts whirl and call—
　We are down a-dabbling
　Up tails all!

THE COW

Robert Louis Stevenson (1850–1894)

THE friendly cow all red and white,
    I love with all my heart:
She gives me cream with all her might,
    To eat with apple-tart.

She wanders lowing here and there,
    And yet she cannot stray,
All in the pleasant open air,
    The pleasant light of day;

And blown by all the winds that pass
    And wet with all the showers,
She walks among the meadow grass
    And eats the meadow flowers.

THE MOWER TO THE GLOW-WORMS

Andrew Marvell (1621–1678)

YE living lamps, by whose dear light
The nightingale does sit so late,
And studying all the summer night,
Her matchless songs does meditate;

Ye country comets, that portend
No war nor prince's funeral,
Shining unto no higher end
Than to presage the grass's fall;

Ye glow-worms, whose officious flame
To wandering mowers shows the way,
That in the night have lost their aim,
And after foolish fires do stray;

Your courteous lights in vain you waste,
Since Juliana here is come,
For she my mind hath so displaced
That I shall never find my home.

THE WHITE OWL

Alfred, Lord Tennyson (1809–1892)

WHEN cats run home and light is come,
    And dew is cold upon the ground,
And the far-off stream is dumb,
    And the whirring sail goes round,
    And the whirring sail goes round;
      Alone and warming his five wits,
      The white owl in the belfry sits.

When merry milkmaids click the latch,
    And rarely smells the new-mown hay,
And the cock hath sung beneath the thatch
    Twice or thrice his roundelay,
    Twice or thrice his roundelay;
      Alone and warming his five wits,
      The white owl in the belfry sits.

THE VIXEN

John Clare (1793–1864)

AMONG the taller wood with ivy hung,
The old fox plays and dances round her young.
She snuffs and barks if any passes by
And swings her tail and turns prepared to fly.
The horseman hurries by, she bolts to see,
And turns again, from danger never free.
If any stands she runs among the poles
And barks and snaps and drives them in the holes.
The shepherd sees them and the boy goes by
And gets a stick and progs the hole to try.
They get all still and lie in safety sure,
And out again when everything's secure,
And start and snap at blackbirds bouncing by
To fight and catch the great white butterfly.

HORSE OF WESTBURY

Charles Tennyson Turner (1808–1879)

AS from the Dorset shore I travelled home,
    I saw the charger of the Wiltshire wold;
    A far-seen figure, stately to behold,
Whose groom the shepherd is, the hoe his comb;
His wizard-spell even sober daylight owned;
    That night I dreamed him into living will;
    He neighed—and, straight, the chalk poured down the hill;
He shook himself, and all beneath was stoned;

Hengist and Horsa shouted o'er my sleep,
    Like fierce Achilles; while that storm-blanched horse
    Sprang to the van of all the Saxon force,
And pushed the Britons to the Western deep;
    Then, dream-wise, as it were a thing of course,
He floated upwards, and regained the steep.

MY HORSES

Traditional

I ONCE was a bold fellow and went with a team,
And all my delight was a-keeping them clean,
With brushes and curries I'd show their bright colour,
And the name that they gave me was 'a hearty good fellow'.

As every evening I go to my bed,
The thought of my horses comes into my head,
I will rise the next morning to give them some meat,
As soon as I can get my shoes on my feet.

The first was a white horse, as white as the milk,
The next was a grey horse, as grey as the silk,
The next was a black horse, as sleek as a mole,
The next was a brown horse, like diamonds did show.

As I go a-driving all on the highway,
When light goes my load, then I feed them with hay,
And give them some water when we come to a pond,
And after they've drunk, boys, go steady along.

My feet they grow weary walking by their side;
I said to my mate, 'I will get up and ride,'
And as I was riding I made a new song,
And as I did sing it you must learn it a-long.

BOB'S LANE

Edward Thomas   (1878-1917)

WOMEN he liked, did shovel-bearded Bob,
Old Farmer Hayward of the Heath, but he
Loved horses. He himself was like a cob
And leather-coloured. Also he loved a tree.

For the life in them he loved most living things,
But a tree chiefly. All along the lane
He planted elms where now the stormcock sings
That travellers hear from the slow-climbing train.

Till then the track had never had a name
For all its thicket and the nightingales
That should have earned it. No one was to blame
To name a thing beloved man sometimes fails.

Many years since, Bob Hayward died, and now
None passes there because the mist and the rain
Out of the elms have turned the lane to slough
And gloom, the name alone survives, Bob's Lane.

from **THE SCHOLAR GYPSY**

Matthew Arnold (1822–1888)

*G*O, for they call you, shepherd, from the hill!
   Go, shepherd, and untie the wattled cotes!
     No longer leave thy wistful flock unfed,
   Nor let thy bawling fellows rack their throats,
   Nor the cropped grasses shoot another head!
     But when the fields are still,
   And the tired men and dogs all gone to rest,
   And only the white sheep are sometimes seen
     Cross and recross the strips of moon-blanched green,
Come, shepherd, and again begin the quest!

Here, where the reaper was at work of late—
   In this high field's dark corner, where he leaves
     His coat, his basket, and his earthen cruse,
   And in the sun all morning binds the sheaves,
   Then here, at noon, comes back his stores to use—
     Here will I sit and wait,
   While to my ear from uplands far away
   The bleating of the folded flocks is borne,
     With distant cries of reapers in the corn—
All the live murmur of a summer's day.

THE THRESHER'S LABOUR

Stephen Duck (1705–1756)

YE reapers, cast your eyes around the field;
And view the various scenes its beauties yield.
Then look again, with a more tender eye,
To think how soon it must in ruin lie!
For, once set in, where-e'er our blows we deal,
There's no resisting of the well-whet steel:
But here or there, where-e'er our course we bend,
Sure desolation does our steps attend …
The morning past, we sweat beneath the sun;
And but uneasily our work goes on.
Before us we perplexing thistles find,
And corn blown adverse with the ruffling wind.
Behind our master waits; and if he spies
One charitable ear, he grudging cries,
'Ye scatter half your wages o'er the land.'
Then scrapes the stubble with his greedy hand.
Let those who feast at ease on dainty fare,
Pity the reapers, who their feasts prepare;
For toils scarce ever ceasing press us now;
Rest never does, but on the Sabbath, show;
And barely that our masters will allow.

Think what a painful life we daily lead;
Each morning early rise, go late to bed:
Nor, when asleep, are we secure from pain;
We then perform our labours o'er again:
Our mimic fancy ever restless seems;
And what we act awake, she acts in dreams.
Hard fate! Our labours ev'n in sleep don't cease;
Scarce Hercules e'er felt such toils as these!
But soon we rise the bearded crop again,
Soon Phoebus' rays well dry the golden grain.
Pleased with the scene, our master glows with joy;
Bids us for carrying all our force employ;
When straight confusion o'er the field appears,
And stunning clamours fill the workmen's ears;
The bells and clashing whips alternate sound,
And rattling waggons thunder o'er the ground.
The wheat, when carried, pease, and other grain,
We soon secure, and leave a fruitless plain;
In noisy triumph the last load moves on,
And loud huzzas proclaim the harvest done.

THE FARMER

Anon

LET the wealthy and great
Roll in splendour and state,;
    I envy them not, I declare it.
I eat my own lamb,
My own chickens and ham;
    I shear my own fleece and I wear it.
I have lawns, I have bowers,
I have fruits, I have flowers,
    The lark is my morning alarmer.
So jolly boys now
Here's God speed the plough,
    Long life, and success to the farmer!

ODE ON SOLITUDE

Alexander Pope (1688–1744)

HAPPY the man whose wish and care
  A few paternal acres bound,
Content to breathe his native air,
      In his own ground.

Whose herds with milk, whose fields with bread,
  Whose flocks supply him with attire,
Whose trees in summer yield him shade,
      In winter, fire.

Blest, who can unconcernedly find
  Hours, days, and years slide soft away,
In health of body, peace of mind,
      Quiet by day,

Sound sleep by night; study and ease
  Together mixed; sweet recreation;
And innocence, which most does please
      With meditation.

Thus let me live, unseen, unknown,
  Thus unlamented let me die,
Steal from the world, and not a stone
      Tell where I lie.

THE VILLAGE BLACKSMITH

Henry Wadsworth Longfellow (1807–1882)

UNDER a spreading chestnut-tree
　　The village smithy stands;
The smith, a mighty man is he,
　　With large and sinewy hands;
And the muscles of his brawny arms
　　Are strong as iron bands.

His hair is crisp, and black, and long,
　　His face is like the tan;
His brow is wet with honest sweat,
　　He earns whate'er he can,
And looks the whole world in the face,
　　For he owes not any man.

Week in, week out, from morn till night,
　　You can hear his bellows blow;
You can hear him swing his heavy sledge,
　　With measured beat and slow,
Like a sexton ringing the village bell,
　　When the evening sun is low.

And children coming home from school
　　Look in at the open door;
They love to see the flaming forge,
　　And hear the bellows roar,
And catch the burning sparks that fly
　　Like chaff from a threshing-floor …

Toiling,—rejoicing,—sorrowing,
　　Onward through life he goes;
Each morning sees some task begin,
　　Each evening sees it close;
Something attempted, something done,
　　Has earned a night's repose.

Thanks, thanks to thee, my worthy friend,
　　For the lesson thou hast taught!
Thus at the flaming forge of life
　　Our fortunes must be wrought;
Thus on its sounding anvil shaped
　　Each burning deed and thought.

from THE DESERTED VILLAGE

Oliver Goldsmith (1730–1774)

SWEET Auburn, loveliest village of the plain,
Where health and plenty cheered the labouring swain,
Where smiling spring its earliest visits paid,
And parting summer's lingering blooms delayed.
Dear lovely bowers of innocence and ease,
Seats of my youth, when every sport could please,
How often have I loitered o'er thy green,
Where humble happiness endeared each scene!
How often have I paused on every charm,
The sheltered cot, the cultivated farm,
The never-failing brook, the busy mill,
The decent church that topped the neighbouring hill,
The hawthorn bush, with seats beneath the shade,
For talking age and whispering lovers made!
How often have I blessed the coming day,
When toil remitting lent its turn to play,
And all the village train, from labour free,
Led up their sports beneath the spreading tree,
While many a pastime circled in the shade,

The young contending as the old surveyed;
And many a gambol frolicked o'er the ground,
And sleights of art and feats of strength went round;
And still as each repeated pleasure tired,
Succeeding sports the mirthful band inspired:
The dancing pair that simply sought renown,
By holding out to tire each other down …

Sweet was the sound, when oft, at evening's close
Up yonder hill the village murmur rose;
There, as I passed with careless steps and slow,
The mingling notes came softened from below:
The swain responsive as the milk-maid sung,
The sober herd that lowed to meet their young:
The noisy geese that gabbled o'er the pool,
The playful children just let loose from school;
The watchdog's voice that bayed the whispering wind,
And the loud laugh that spoke the vacant mind …

NURSE'S SONG

William Blake (1757–1827)

WHEN the voices of children are heard on the green,
   And laughing is heard on the hill,
My heart is at rest within my breast,
   And everything else is still.

'Then come home, my children, the sun is gone down,
   And the dews of night arise;
Come, come, leave off play, and let us away
   Till the morning appears in the skies.'

'No, no, let us play, for it is yet day,
   And we cannot go to sleep;
Besides, in the sky the little birds fly,
   And the hills are all covered with sheep.'

'Well, well, go and play till the light fades away,
   And then go home to bed.'
The little ones leaped and shouted and laughed
   And all the hills echoèd.

REST

Margaret L Woods (1856–?)

To spend the long warm days
   Silent beside the silent-stealing streams,
     To see, not gaze,
   To hear, not listen, thoughts exchanged for dreams:

     See clouds that slowly pass
   Trailing their shadows o'er the far faint down,
     And ripening grass,
   While yet the meadows wear their starry crown.

     To hear the breezes sigh
   Cool in the silver leaves like falling rain,
     Pause and go by,
   Tired wanderers o'er the solitary plain:

     See far from all affright
   Shy river creatures play hour after hour,
     And night by night
   Low in the west the white moon's folding flower.

     Thus lost to human things,
   To blend at last with Nature and to hear
     What songs she sings
   Low to herself when there is no one near.

THE LIGHT OF OTHER DAYS

Thomas Moore (1779–1852)

OFT in the stilly night,
    Ere slumber's chain has bound me,
Fond Memory brings the light
    Of other days around me:
      The smiles, the tears
      Of boyhood's years,
    The words of love then spoken;
      The eyes that shone,
      Now dimmed and gone,
    The cheerful hearts now broken!
Thus, in the stilly night,
    Ere slumber's chain has bound me,
Sad Memory brings the light
    Of other days around me.

When I remember all
    The friends so linked together
I've seen around me fall
    Like leaves in wintry weather,
      I feel like one
      Who treads alone
    Some banquet-hall deserted,
      Whose lights are fled,
      Whose garlands dead,
    And all but he departed!
Thus in the stilly night,
    Ere slumber's chain has bound me,
Sad Memory brings the light
    Of other days around me.

from ELEGY WRITTEN IN A COUNTRY CHURCHYARD

Thomas Gray (1716–1771)

THE curfew tolls the knell of parting day,
    The lowing herd wind slowly o'er the lea,
The ploughman homeward plods his weary way,
    And leaves the world to darkness, and to me.

Now fades the glimmering landscape on the sight,
    And all the air a solemn stillness holds,
Save where the beetle wheels his droning flight,
    And drowsy tinklings lull the distant folds:

Save that from yonder ivy-mantled tower
    The moping owl does to the moon complain
Of such as, wandering near her secret bower,
    Molest her ancient solitary reign.

Beneath those rugged elms, that yew-tree's shade,
    Where heaves the turf in many a mouldering heap,
Each in his narrow cell forever laid,
    The rude Forefathers of the hamlet sleep.

The breezy call of incense-breathing morn,
    The swallow twittering from the straw-built shed,
The cock's shrill clarion, or the echoing horn,
    No more shall rouse them from their lowly bed.

For them no more the blazing hearth shall burn,
    Or busy housewife ply her evening care:
No children run to lisp their sire's return,
    Or climb his knees the envied kiss to share.

Oft did the harvest to their sickle yield,
    Their furrow oft the stubborn glebe has broke;
How jocund did they drive their team afield!
    How bowed the woods beneath their sturdy stroke!

Let not Ambition mock their useful toil,
    Their homely joys, and destiny obscure;
Nor Grandeur hear with a disdainful smile
    The short and simple annals of the Poor …

TO MEADOWS

Robert Herrick (1591–1674)

YE have been fresh and green,
    Ye have been filled with flowers,
And ye the walks have been
    Where maids have spent their hours.

You have beheld how they
    With wicker arks did come
To kiss, and bear away
    The richer cowslips home.

You've heard them sweetly sing,
    And seen them in a round,
Each virgin like a spring
    With honeysuckles crowned.

But now we see none here
    Whose silvery feet did tread
And with dishevelled hair
    Adorned this smoother mead.

Like unthrifts having spent
    Your stock, and needy grown,
You're left here to lament
    Your poor estates alone.

TO AUTUMN

John Keats (1795–1821)

SEASON of mists and mellow fruitfulness,
 Close bosom-friend of the maturing sun;
Conspiring with him how to load and bless
 With fruit the vines that round the thatch-eaves run;
To bend with apples the mossed cottage-trees,
 And fill all fruit with ripeness to the core;
  To swell the gourd, and plump the hazel shells
 With a sweet kernel; to set budding more,
And still more, later flowers for the bees,
Until they think warm days will never cease;
  For Summer has o'er-brimmed their clammy cells.

Who hath not seen thee oft amid thy store?
 Sometimes whoever seeks abroad may find
Thee sitting careless on a granary floor,
 Thy hair soft-lifted by the winnowing wind;
Or on a half-reaped furrow sound asleep,
 Drowsed with the fume of poppies, while thy hook

Spares the next swath and all its twinèd flowers;
And sometimes like a gleaner thou dost keep
 Steady thy laden head across a brook;
 Or by a cyder-press, with patient look,
  Thou watchest the last oozings, hours by hours.

Where are the songs of Spring? Aye, where are they?
 Think not of them,—thou hast thy music too,
While barrèd clouds bloom the soft-dying day
 And touch the stubble-plains with rosy hue;
Then in a wailful choir the small gnats mourn
 Among the river sallows, borne aloft
  Or sinking as the light wind lives or dies;
And full-grown lambs loud bleat from hilly bourn;
 Hedge-crickets sing, and now with treble soft
 The redbreast whistles from a garden-croft,
  And gathering swallows twitter in the skies.

from THE GARDENER'S DAUGHTER

Alfred, Lord Tennyson (1809–1892)

*N*OT wholly in the busy world, nor quite
Beyond it, blooms the garden that I love.
News from the humming city comes to it
In sound of funeral or of marriage bells;
And, sitting muffled in dark leaves, you hear
The windy clanging of the minster clock;
Although between it and the garden lies
A league of grass, washed by a slow broad stream,
That, stirred with languid pulses of the oar,
Waves all its lazy lilies, and creeps on,
Barge-laden, to three arches of a bridge
Crowned with the minster-towers. The fields between
Are dewy-fresh, browsed by deep-uddered kine,
And all about the large lime feathers low,
The lime a summer home of murmurous wings.

SOWING

Edward Thomas (1878–1917)

IT was a perfect day
For sowing; just
As sweet and dry was the ground
As tobacco-dust.

I tasted deep the hour
Between the far
Owl's chuckling first soft cry
And the first star.

A long stretched hour it was;
Nothing undone
Remained; the early seeds
All safely sown.

And now, hark at the rain,
Windless and light,
Half a kiss, half a tear,
Saying good-night.

from REFLECTIONS ON HAVING LEFT A PLACE OF RETIREMENT

Samuel Taylor Coleridge (1772–1834)

LOW was our pretty cot: our tallest rose
Peeped at the chamber-window. We could hear
At silent noon, and eve, and early morn,
The sea's faint murmur. In the open air
Our myrtles blossomed; and across the porch
Thick jasmins twined: the little landscape round
Was green and woody, and refreshed the eye.
It was a spot which you might aptly call
The Valley of Seclusion! Once I saw
(Hallowing his Sabbath-day by quietness)
A wealthy son of commerce saunter by,
Bristowa's citizen: methought, it calmed
His thirst of idle gold, and made him muse
With wiser feelings: for he paused, and looked
With a pleased sadness, and gazed all around,
Then eyed our cottage, and gazed round again,
And sighed, and said, it was a blessed place.
And we *were* blessed. Oft with patient ear

Long-listening to the viewless skylark's note
(Viewless, or haply for a moment seen
Gleaming on sunny wings) in whispered tones
I've said to my beloved, 'Such, sweet girl!
The inobtrusive song of happiness,
Unearthly minstrelsy! then only heard
When the soul seeks to hear; when all is hushed,
And the heart listens!' ...

Yet oft when after honourable toil
Rests the tired mind, and waking loves to dream,
My spirit shall revisit thee, dear cot!
Thy jasmin and thy window-peeping rose,
And myrtles fearless of the mild sea-air.
And I shall sigh fond wishes—sweet abode!
Ah!—had none greater! And that all had such!
It might be so—but the time is not yet.
Speed it, O Father! Let thy Kingdom come!

THE POPLAR-FIELD

William Cowper (1731–1800)

THE poplars are felled; farewell to the shade
And the whispering sound of the cool colonnade;
The winds play no longer and sing in the leaves,
Nor Ouse on his bosom their image receives.

Twelve years have elapsed since I first took a view
Of my favourite field, and the bank where they grew:
And now in the grass behold they are laid,
And the tree is my seat that once lent me a shade.

The blackbird has fled to another retreat,
Where the hazels afford him a screen from the heat;
And the scene where his melody charmed me before
Resounds with his sweet-flowing ditty no more.

My fugitive years are all hasting away,
And I must ere long lie as lowly as they,
With a turf on my breast, and a stone at my head,
Ere another such grove shall arise in its stead.

'Tis a sight to engage me, if anything can,
To muse on the perishing pleasures of man;
Though his life be a dream, his enjoyments, I see,
Have a being less durable even than he.

WOODMAN, SPARE THAT TREE!

George Pope Morris (1802-1864)

WOODMAN, spare that tree!
 Touch not a single bough!
In youth it sheltered me,
 And I'll protect it now.
'Twas my forefather's hand
 That placed it near his cot;
There, woodman, let it stand,
 Thy axe shall harm it not.

That old familiar tree,
 Whose glory and renown
Are spread o'er land and sea—
 And wouldst thou hew it down?
Woodman, forbear thy stroke!
 Cut not its earth-bound ties;
Oh, spare that aged oak
 Now towering to the skies.

When but an idle boy
 I sought its grateful shade;
In all their gushing joy
 Here too my sisters played.
My mother kissed me here;
 My father pressed my hand—
Forgive this foolish tear,
 But let that old oak stand!

My heart-strings round thee cling,
 Close as thy bark, old friend!
Here shall the wild-bird sing,
 And still thy branches bend.
Old tree! the storm still brave!
 And, woodman, leave the spot;
While I've a hand to save,
 Thy axe shall harm it not.

DARTSIDE

Charles Kingsley (1819–1875)

I CANNOT tell what you say, green leaves,
    I cannot tell what you say:
  But I know that there is a spirit in you,
    And a word in you this day.

I cannot tell what you say, rosy rocks,
    I cannot tell what you say:
  But I know that there is a spirit in you,
    And a word in you this day.

I cannot tell what you say, brown streams,
    I cannot tell what you say:
  But I know that in you too a spirit doth live,
    And a word doth speak this day.

'Oh green is the colour of faith and truth,
And rose the colour of love and youth,
    And brown of the fruitful clay.
Sweet Earth is faithful, and fruitful, and young,
    And her bridal day shall come ere long,
And you shall know what the rocks and the streams
    And the whispering woodlands say.'

WEATHERS

Thomas Hardy (1840–1928)

THIS is the weather the cuckoo likes,
    And so do I;
When showers betumble the chestnut spikes,
    And nestlings fly:
And the little brown nightingale bills his best,
And they sit outside at 'The Traveller's Rest',
And maids come forth sprig-muslin drest,
And citizens dream of the south and west,
    And so do I.

This is the weather the shepherd shuns,
    And so do I;
When beeches drip in browns and duns,
    And thresh, and ply;
And hill-hid tides throb, throe on throe,
And meadow rivulets overflow,
And drops on gate-bars hang in a row,
And rooks in families homeward go,
    And so do I.

WHEN ICICLES HANG BY THE WALL

William Shakespeare (1564–1616)

WHEN icicles hang by the wall
    And Dick the shepherd blows his nail
And Tom bears logs into the hall,
    And milk comes frozen home in pail,
When blood is nipt, and ways be foul,
Then nightly sings the staring owl
      Tuwhoo!
Tuwhit! tuwhoo! A merry note!
While greasy Joan doth keel the pot.

When all aloud the wind doth blow,
    And coughing drowns the parson's saw,
And birds sit brooding in the snow,
    And Marian's nose looks red and raw:
When roasted crabs hiss in the bowl—
Then nightly sings the staring owl
      Tuwhoo!
Tuwhit! tuwhoo! A merry note!
While greasy Joan doth keel the pot.

WINTER

Alfred, Lord Tennyson (1809–1892)

THE frost is here,
And fuel is dear,
And woods are sear,
And fires burn clear,
And frost is here
And has bitten the heel of the going year.

Bite, frost, bite!
You roll up away from the light
The blue wood-louse, and the plump dormouse,
And the bees are stilled, and the flies are killed,
And you bite far into the heart of the house,
But not into mine.

Bite, frost, bite!
The woods are all the searer,
The fuel is all the dearer,
The fires are all the clearer,
My spring is all the nearer,
You have bitten into the heart of the earth,
But not into mine.

SONG OF THE YEAR

Edward Fitzgerald (1809–1893)

TIS a dull sight
　　To see the year dying,
When winter winds
　　Set the yellow wood sighing:
　　　　Sighing, O sighing!

When such a time cometh,
　　I do retire
Into an old room
　　Beside a bright fire:
　　　　O, pile a bright fire!

And there I sit
　　Reading old things,
Of knights and lorn damsels,
　　While the wind sings—
　　　　O, drearily sings!

I never look out
　　Nor attend to the blast:
For all to be seen
　　Is the leaves falling fast:
　　　　Falling, falling!

But close at the hearth,
　　Like a cricket, sit I,
Reading of summer
　　And chivalry—
　　　　Gallant chivalry!

Then with an old friend
　　I talk of our youth—
How 'twas gladsome, but often
　　Foolish, forsooth:
　　　　But gladsome, gladsome!

Or, to get merry,
　　We sing some old rhyme,
That made the wood ring again
　　In summer time—
　　　　Sweet summer time!

Then go we smoking,
　　Silent and snug:
Naught passes between us,
　　Save a brown jug—
　　　　Sometimes!

And sometimes a tear
　　Will rise in each eye,
Seeing the two old friends
　　So merrily—
　　　　So merrily! …

Thus, then, live I
　　Till, 'mid all the gloom,
By Heaven! the bold sun
　　Is with me in the room
　　　　Shining, shining!

Then the clouds part,
　　Swallows soaring between;
The spring is alive,
　　And the meadows are green!

I jump up, like mad,
　　Break the old pipe in twain,
And away to the meadows,
　　The meadows again!

HOME-THOUGHTS FROM ABROAD

Robert Browning (1812–1889)

OH, to be in England
Now that April's there,
And whoever wakes in England
Sees, some morning, unaware,
That the lowest boughs and the brushwood sheaf
Round the elm-tree bole are in tiny leaf,
While the chaffinch sings on the orchard bough
    In England—now!

  And after April, when May follows,
And the whitethroat builds, and all the swallows!
Hark, where my blossomed pear-tree in the hedge
  Leans to the field and scatters on the clover
Blossoms and dewdrops—at the bent spray's edge—
  That's the wise thrush; he sings each song twice over,
Lest you should think he never could recapture
  The first fine careless rapture!
And though the fields look rough with hoary dew,
All will be gay when noontide wakes anew
The buttercups, the little children's dower
—Far brighter than this gaudy melon-flower!

from THE OLD VICARAGE, GRANTCHESTER

Rupert Brooke (1887–1915)

JUST now the lilac is in bloom,
All before my little room;
And in my flower-beds, I think,
Smile the carnation and the pink;
And down the borders, well I know,
The poppy and the pansy blow …
Oh! there the chestnuts, summer through,
Beside the river make for you
A tunnel of green gloom, and sleep
Deeply above; and green and deep
The stream mysterious glides beneath,
Green as a dream and deep as death.
—Oh, damn! I know it! and I know
How the May fields all golden show,
And when the day is young and sweet,
Gild gloriously the bare feet
That run to bathe …

Ah God! to see the branches stir

Across the moon at Grantchester!
To smell the thrilling-sweet and rotten
Unforgettable, unforgotten
River-smell, and hear the breeze
Sobbing in the little trees.
Say, do the elm-clumps greatly stand
Still guardians of that holy land?
The chestnuts shade, in reverend dream,
The yet unacademic stream? …
Oh, is the water sweet and cool,
Gentle and brown, above the pool?
And laughs the immortal river still
Under the mill, under the mill?
Say, is there Beauty yet to find?
And Certainty? and Quiet kind?
Deep meadows yet, for to forget
The lies, and truths, and pain? … oh! yet
Stands the Church clock at ten to three?
And is there honey still for tea?

from RICHARD II

William Shakespeare (1564–1616)

THIS royal throne of kings, this sceptred isle,
This earth of majesty, this seat of Mars,
This other Eden, demi-paradise,
This fortress built by Nature for herself
Against infection and the hand of war,
This happy breed of men, this little world,
This precious stone set in the silver sea,
Which serves it in the office of a wall
Or as a moat defensive to a house,
Against the envy of less happier lands,—
This blessed plot, this earth, this realm, this England.

JERUSALEM

William Blake (1757–1827)

AND did those feet in ancient time
Walk upon England's mountains green?
And was the holy Lamb of God
On England's pleasant pastures seen?

And did the Countenance Divine
Shine forth upon our clouded hills?
And was Jerusalem builded here
Among these dark Satanic mills?

Bring me my bow of burning gold:
Bring me my arrows of desire:
Bring me my spear: O clouds unfold!
Bring me my chariot of fire.

I will not cease from mental fight,
Nor shall my sword sleep in my hand
Till we have built Jerusalem
In England's green and pleasant land.

PHOTO INFORMATION

INDEX